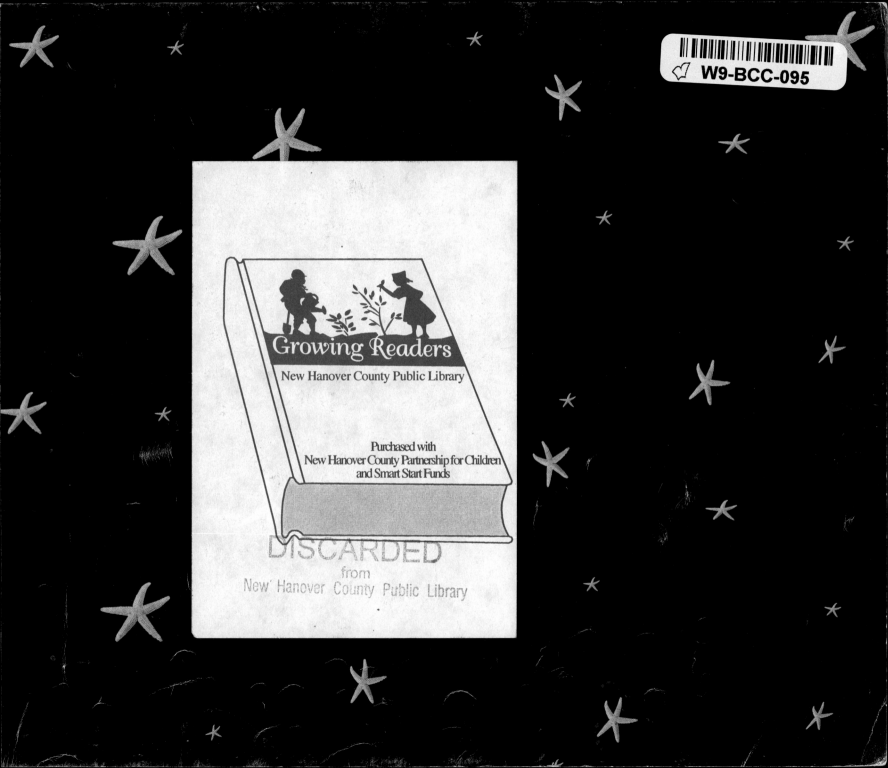

This Is the Rain

by **LOLA M. SCHAEFER**

illustrated by **JANE WATTENBERG**

GREENWILLOW BOOKS
An Imprint of HarperCollinsPublishers

that warms the ocean,
blue and vast,
that holds the rainwater from the past.

This is the vapor,

moist and light,
made when sunshine,
hot and bright,
warms the ocean,
blue and vast,

that holds the rainwater from the past.

that holds the rainwater from the past.

These are the clouds,
low and gray,
full of vapor, moist and light,
made when **sunshine,**
hot and bright,
warms the ocean,
blue and vast,

This is the rain,

falling all day,
    that forms in clouds,
        low and gray,
    full of vapor, moist and light,

made when sunshine,
    hot and bright,

    warms the ocean, blue and vast,

that holds the rainwater from the past.

This is the land,
dry, porous ground

that absorbs the rain, falling all day,
that forms in clouds, low and gray,
full of vapor, moist and light,
made when sunshine, hot and bright,
warms the ocean, blue and vast,

that holds the rainwater
from the past.

These are the puddles,
big and round,
that dot the land, muddy, wet ground

that absorbed the rain, falling all day,
that formed in clouds, low and gray,
full of vapor, moist and light,
made when

sunshine,
hot and bright,

warms the ocean, blue and vast,

that holds the rainwater from the past.

This is the water,
seeking low ground,
that runs into ditches

that pour into creeks

that drain into rivers

The Water Cycle on the Planet Earth

The water cycle is a natural process that continually moves water between the oceans and the land. Because it keeps the water in lakes and rivers fresh, the water cycle makes life on land possible.

The heat of the sun evaporates, or picks up, water from the oceans and other wet surfaces on Earth. Fresh water rises into the air as invisible vapor, and salt and other minerals from the oceans are left behind. As the vapor rises higher, it cools and condenses into tiny water droplets. The droplets are light enough to float in the air, and they collect to form clouds. Water then falls back to Earth as rain, sleet, hail, or snow. Plants and animals use some of this fresh water to live. The rest of the water either seeps into the land to form underground wells and springs, or flows back to the rivers, lakes, and oceans.

For Derek, who loves to
know how and why —L.S.

For Betsey—in rain or shine —J.W.

Special thanks to Gideon and Solomon Chase,
my very best all-weather critics and advisers.
And many thanks to Isaiah Chase, for his fine
photos of the unusual blue-footed booby and
the sun-burned Galápagos crabs. And to
Samuel, my gentle sea breeze.

The heavens are shining on an extraordinary
triumvirate. A roaring waterfall of appreciation
and affection for Virginia Duncan, Ava Weiss,
and Susan Hirschman. —J.W.

The illustrations are a blend of photographs and original imagery
collaged on the computer using Adobe Photoshop™.
The typeface is Kabel.

Library of Congress Cataloging-in-Publication Data
Schaefer, Lola M., (date)
This is the rain / by Lola M. Schaefer ; illustrated by
Jane Wattenberg.
   p.   cm.
"Greenwillow Books."
Summary: Cumulative text describes how water falls from
the clouds as rain and eventually makes its way to the sea.
ISBN 0-688-17039-0 (trade). ISBN 0-688-17040-4 (lib. bdg.)
[1. Rain and rainfall—Fiction. 2. Hydrologic cycle—Fiction.
3. Water—Fiction. 4. Stories in rhyme.]   I. Wattenberg, Jane, ill.
II. Title. PZ8.3.S289 Th 2001 [E]—dc21 00-062226

1 2 3 4 5 6 7 8 9 10   First Edition